STARTING BLUEGRASS BANJO

By Robin Roller

Oak Publications

Music Sales America

DISTRIBUTED BY

HAL•LEONARD®
CORPORATION
7777 W. BLUEMOUND RD. P.O. BOX 13819 MILWAUKEE, WI 53213

Project editor: Felipe Orozco
Interior design and layout: Len Vogler
Cover design: Stacy Boge

Order No. OK65120
ISBN 10: 0.8256.0352.8
ISBN 13: 978.0.8256.0352.5

CONTENTS

CD TRACK LIST

1. Tuning
2. Getting Used to the Strings
3. Roll 1—Thumb In and Out
4. Roll 2—Forward-Backward Roll
5. Roll 3—Forward Roll
6. Roll 4—Backward Roll
7. Roll 5—Alternate Forward-Backward Roll
8. Roll 6—Fill-In Roll
9. Roll 7—Alternating Thumb Pattern
10. Roll 8—Alternate Forward Roll
11. The Pinch/Pluck Technique
12. Thumb In and Out Roll with D7 Chord
13. Forward-Backward Roll with C chord
14. The Slide
15. The Hammer-On
16. The Push-Off
17. The Pull-Off
18. Cripple Creek
19. She'll Be Comin' 'Round the Mountain
20. Hot Corn Cold Corn
21. Old Joe Clark
22. Bill Cheatham
23. Red River Valley
24. Nine Pound Hammer
25. John Hardy

ACKNOWLEDGMENTS

This book wouldn't be possible or even exist if I didn't first thank my Dad, Bob Roller, my first and best teacher, for showing me a roll, and making sure that I played it well and didn't get in a hurry. Secondly, I would have to say thank you to my Mom, Ellen, for putting up with not one, but TWO banjo players in the house, and for her endless encouragement. As well, thank you to my family in Canada for supporting their little sis as she chased her dream.

More thank-yous for their help, support and encouragement go out to D'Arcy Campbell and Hubert Giroux (Crazy Canucks!), Amy and Jeff Murray, Gail Rudisill-Johnson, Carl Caldwell, Ross Jacobsmeyer, Matt and Christy Jones, Dale Wilkes, and Terry Johnson. My endless thanks and gratitude go out to Ricky and Micol Davis for their time with this project and for being the most wonderful neighbors and friends!

FOREWORD

Hi there, and thank you for choosing this instruction book as your introduction to bluegrass banjo. My goal is to provide beginners with an easy-to-read, easy-to-understand tool to learn with and to get you playing—and playing well—as soon as possible. I've been playing the banjo for 24 years, but I still remember learning my first roll like it was yesterday. I was fourteen, and I asked my dad, who was also in the beginning stages of learning and teaching himself, to show me something on the banjo. Learning that first roll and then the next was as exciting to me as anything that I had ever done. About six months after learning that first roll, I got up on stage and played "Foggy Mountain Breakdown" with a real live band and I knew that I had found my place in life.

I moved to Nashville, Tennessee, seventeen years ago, after having spent a year and a half at South Plains Junior College in Levelland, Texas, studying, what else, but bluegrass banjo! I had the great fortune of having banjo teacher extraordinaire Alan Munde as my instructor. Talk about a great teacher! One of the first things that he did was throw away my fingerpicks and give me a set of "real" banjo picks. He certainly set my playing on the straight and narrow in that year and a half, and besides learning how to be a better player, I learned what it took to be a better teacher as well.

In addition to performing professionally in various bluegrass groups, I have taught banjo off and on over the past 22 years—having my own students only two years after I had started playing myself—and have recently started teaching in banjo workshops. I enjoy teaching students who are in the very beginning stages of learning. It is so easy to get on the wrong track when you first start out and I find it very rewarding to be able to help someone get over the rough spots and put them back in the right direction—not to mention that it's very hard to break the bad habits of someone who has played that way for a year or two. This book probably won't be helpful to you if you have been playing for more than six months, as I have directed it toward those who have yet to even put on a set of picks. My style of teaching may be a bit unorthodox, or to some, just plain simple, but over the years I've found that a simple approach for beginners works best. Music can be overwhelming and many say that the banjo is one of the more difficult instruments to play because one hand is doing something completely different from the other, and I feel that the last thing that someone just starting out needs is to be bombarded by unnecessary musical terms and endless tablature. If a student can learn a smooth and well-timed roll, execute left-hand fingering cleanly, and learn to read tablature, then the only thing left for them to do is practice, listen to and watch other banjo players, and they will become good players themselves.

GETTING STARTED

HOW TO USE THIS BOOK

This book was designed as a step-by-step guide to learning how to play the banjo in the easiest and most practical way.

Follow each chapter in a systematic way. If you do so, you'll be playing in no time.

The accompanying CD has a demonstration track for each example, technique, and all of the songs included. The songs are played at both slow and regular tempo, this will help you practice and hear how they should sound.

BANJO PARTS

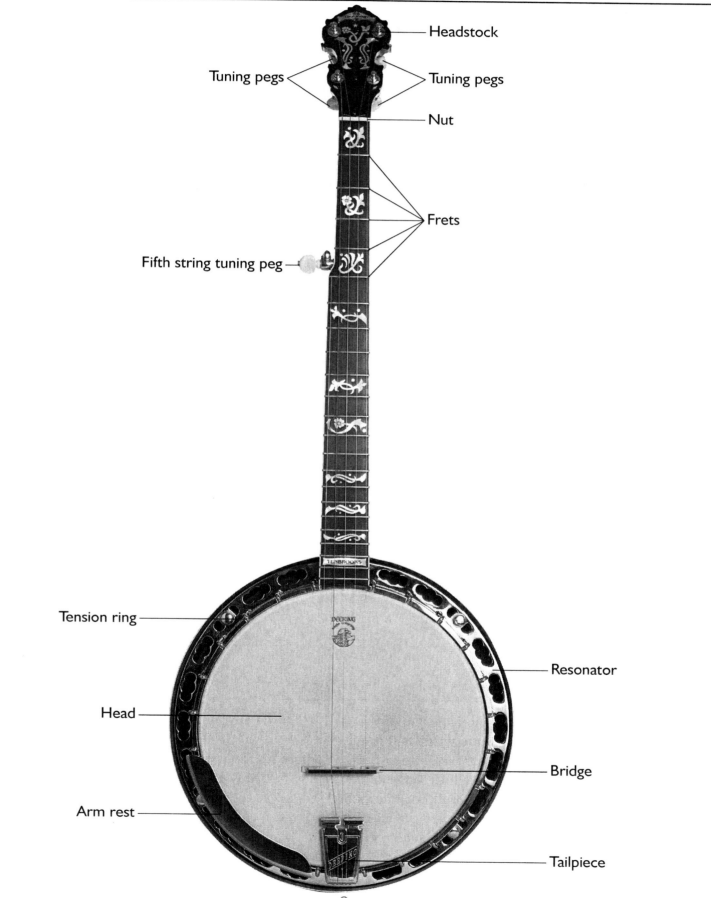

Headstock

Tuning pegs — — Tuning pegs

Nut

Frets

Fifth string tuning peg

Tension ring

Resonator

Head

Bridge

Arm rest

Tailpiece

HOW TO HOLD THE BANJO

One of the most important parts of playing the banjo is holding the instrument properly. Holding it incorrectly can lead to back pain, wrist pain, and shoulder pain—not to mention that it can inhibit technique. I recommend a straight-back chair where your feet can easily rest flat on the floor.

Hold the banjo between your legs with the top of the banjo tilted slightly back. The neck of the banjo should be pointing at an angle of just between 2 and 3 o'clock. A strap will make it easier to keep the banjo in position. Don't bend or lean forward over the instrument.

Sitting Position

Standing Position

PICKS

Wearing Fingerpicks

The fingerpicks go on as shown here. They should fit right over the cuticle part of your fingernail. You don't want them too far up on the tip or too far down on your knuckle. The angle of the pick is often argued but I was told one time—and found that this has worked well for me—that the pick should be a natural extension of your finger. If one finger curves more, then curve that pick a bit more. I have also found that the majority of new finger picks come with angled sides and fit squarely. I like to take a pair of needle-nose pliers and straighten out and then round the sides of the pick to wrap snugly around my finger. I recommend National or Dunlop metal fingerpicks, the stronger the metal, the better, with good resistance. You don't want a metal pick that will bend with the least bit of pressure.

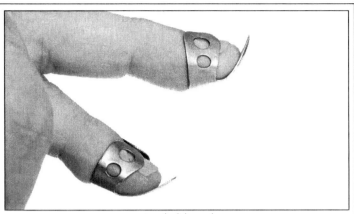

natural pick angles

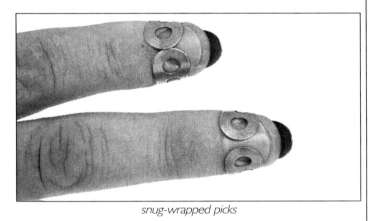

snug-wrapped picks

Thumbpicks

The thumbpick again should fit snugly over the thumb and slightly over the cuticle. If your pick is too big it will turn as you play. A thumbpick can be filed or trimmed if it seems to be hanging up in either the tip or where it wraps around your thumb. Thumbpicks come in plastic or metal but the standard bluegrass banjo player uses a heavy plastic thumbpick. I recommend a National, Dunlop, or Golden Gate, again choosing a heavy one with good resistance that fits snugly on your thumb.

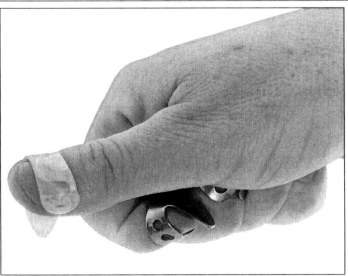

thumbpick slightly over cuticle

RIGHT- AND LEFT-HAND POSITIONING

Right Hand

There is a common argument among banjo players about which is the right way to anchor your right hand on the banjo head. I've seen it done all ways and my answer to this question is: "whatever works for you." Your anchored finger is your right-hand guide so that you'll know where you are positioned on the head without looking while you are paying attention to your left hand.

The most common way is to anchor both the ring and pinky fingers at the bridge:

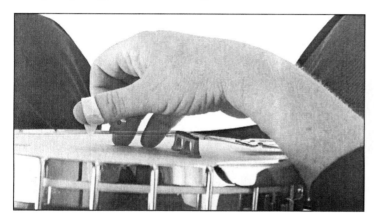

When I first started playing I tried to keep both anchored, but when my ring finger is anchored the rest of my fingers won't move, and so I use my pinky finger for my anchor.

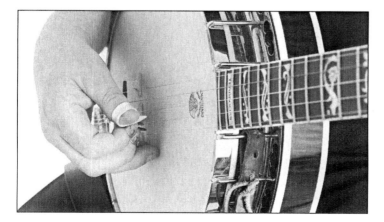

I've seen several great players anchor with just their ring finger anchored and the pinky curled or pointed out. Regardless of which way you find comfortable, the most important thing is to *keep at least one finger anchored*.

Where and how you position your hand when anchoring is another important element. You do not want to press down on the head or rest any finger against the bridge. This will act as a "mute" and dampen or lessen the vibration of the strings. If you have shorter fingers, you may be able to get away with anchoring just in front of the bridge; if you have a larger hand with longer fingers, the best location would be just behind the bottom corner of the bridge. When picking, your fingers should strike just about $3/4$ to 1 inch in front of the bridge. If you find that in the beginning your right hand wanders around on the head a bit, it is perfectly acceptable to put a tiny piece of double-faced tape where your finger should go at the corner of the bridge, and use that to help you anchor.

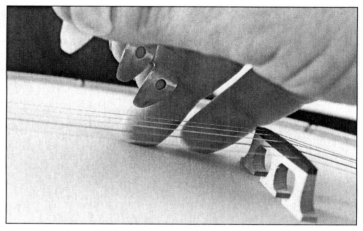

Your wrist should be held at a nice straight angle, not bent or resting against the head.

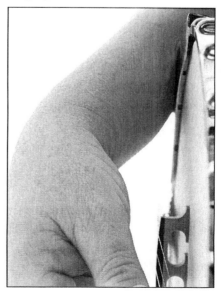

Left Hand

Your left hand should cup the neck of the banjo.

Your wrist should remain straight, but never tense or rigid.

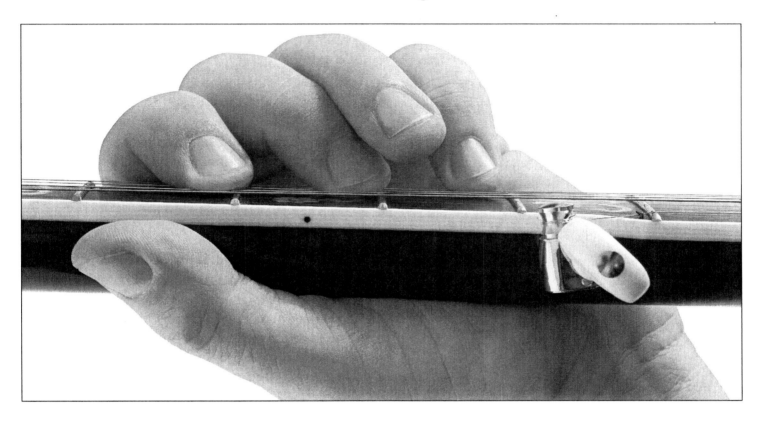

Try not to bend your wrist too far in or too far out.

You don't want your hand to look like the following pictures:

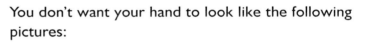
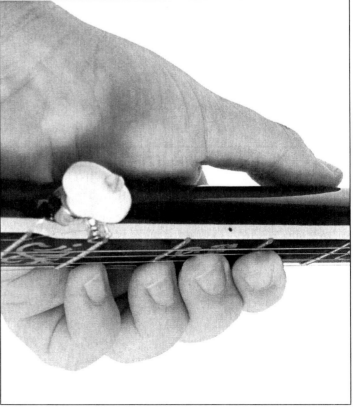

TUNING THE BANJO

Tuning the banjo can often be a difficult task. The out-of-tune banjo has long been the brunt of many musical jokes (refer to joke section at the end of the book). There are different methods of tuning—from pitch pipe to electronic tuner. I would recommend getting an electronic tuner right from the start, as it will lessen tuning time and help you develop your ear for tuning and eliminate the guesswork. There are many different types of tuners in cost and size but you shouldn't have to spend any more than $50 for a very good tuner. I like the Intellitouch Tuner because it picks up all five strings on the banjo equally well. It is not too expensive, it is small, and can clip on the headstock. The Intellitouch Tuner is available at most music stores.

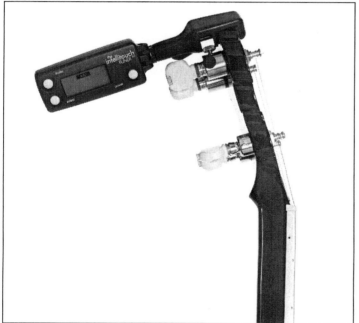

Intellitouch tuner

The banjo is tuned to open G. This is standard bluegrass tuning.

CD Track 4

The fifth string (short one on top) is G, the fourth is D, the third is G, the second is B, and the first (bottom string) is D. The fifth and third strings that are both Gs are one octave apart, the fifth being the higher one. The fourth and first strings that are both Ds are also one octave apart, the first being the higher one.

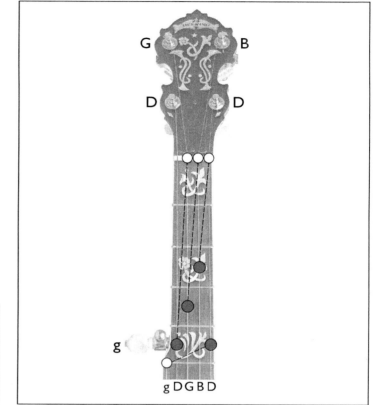

gDGBD

To double-check your tuning after you have tuned to the tuner, you can fret the banjo and match notes by doing the following:

- Play the fourth string at the fifth fret and then play your third string open. They should sound the same.

- Play the third string at the fourth fret and then play your second string open. They should sound the same.

- Play the second string at the third fret and then play the first string open. They should sound the same.

- Play the first string at the fifth fret and then play the fifth string open. They should sound the same.

In doing the above process, tune your fourth string first and go from there. If a string sounds lower than the note you want, it is *flat*. If the string sounds higher than what you want, it is *sharp*.

PICKING THE STRINGS

Let's begin by getting used to hitting the strings.

Place your right hand in the proper position on the banjo head and strum the fifth string with a downward stroke of your thumb:

CD Track 2

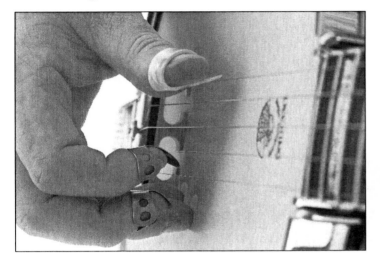

Striking the string with the same intensity each time, continue to strike the fifth string until your thumb feels comfortable. Move onto the other strings using your thumb, striking them repeatedly and evenly. In banjo playing, the thumb will generally strike the fifth through second strings on a regular basis. Rarely will you have to strike the first string (bottom) with your thumb.

Let's move on to the fingers. With your index finger, using an upward motion, strike the third (middle) string. Continue to strike the third string, using the upward motion, with the same intensity each time.

Once your index finger has become comfortable with that string, move on to the second string and do the same exercise, striking it repeatedly, slowly and evenly. The index finger will normally play the second and third strings. There will be occasions when you will use your index finger up on the fourth string or down on the first string, but this is uncommon.

The middle finger is an exception as it will generally only ever play the first (bottom) string. With your middle finger, using an upward motion, strike the first string. Continue striking the first string, slowly and evenly:

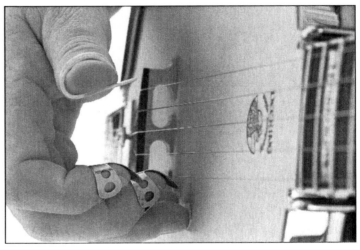

Banjo "tablature" (TAB) is music for the banjo. It is not standard music notation, but would best be described as a "picture" of the strings that are played, along with finger placement and right-hand fingering.

Looking at tablature from the top to bottom, the top string of the TAB is the first (bottom) string on the banjo, the second string from the top of the TAB is the second string from the bottom on the banjo, the middle string on the tablature is the third string on the banjo, and so on.

Tablature for the "getting used to hitting the strings" exercise done earlier (p 15) with the thumb on the third string would look like this:

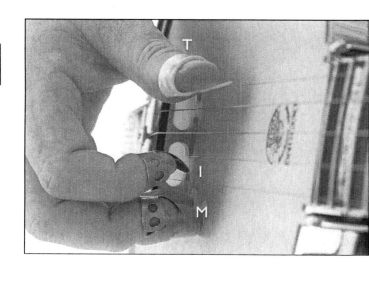

Third string is the one being played.

0 means that the string is being played open, with no left-hand fingering.

These letters refer to which right-hand finger is playing that string.

T = Thumb **I** = Index **M** = Middle

Time Signature

However, while the TAB notations are not actual music notes, they *are* musical timing. Most bluegrass tunes are in $\frac{2}{4}$ or $\frac{4}{4}$ time, therefore the notations will be in either whole, half, quarter, eighth, or sixteenth notes. The standard eight-note banjo roll consists of eight eighth notes. The section of timing that these notes are in is called a "measure."

A typical bluegrass song is usually in $\frac{4}{4}$ time and so there will be four beats per measure and eight notes per four beats. If you were to count $\frac{4}{4}$ time and play along with it, you would count "1 and 2 and 3 and 4 and" while playing notes on the numbers and the "ands." If you were to count and play in $\frac{2}{4}$ time, you would have to count and play "1 and 2 and."

Left-Hand Fingering

The letters above the tablature indicate left-hand fingering: **I**=index, **M**=middle, **R**=ring, and **P**=pinky. The numbers on the line indicate the fret at which you will note the string.

Notes and Rests

Half notes are joined by a tie.
Quarter notes have a single stem.

Half-note rests are placed on the third line. Quarter-note rests are placed in the middle of the TAB.

Eighth Notes and Count

Eighth-note stems will be attached by a single beam at the bottom. In $\frac{4}{4}$ time format, each of these notes would be played two per beat. The timing is indicated by the numbers above the measure and can be played by counting out loud "1 and 2 and 3 and 4 and" with notes being played on the "number" and the "and."

Slide

A straight line between two notes indicates a *slide*. The string is struck on the first note and then slid to the next.

Hammer-On

A curved line above two notes indicates a *hammer-on*. Fret the string with the index finger of your left hand, pluck the string and then, while the note is still ringing, hammer down with your middle finger to create the next note.

Push-Off or Pull-Off

A curved line under two notes indicates a *push-off* or *pull-off*. For the push-off, the string is fretted with the middle finger of your left hand and then released by pushing the string up in a flicking motion. For the pull-off, release in a downward-flicking motion. You can choose to play the pull-off or push-off when you see the symbol (⌣).

17

THE BANJO ROLL

Banjo playing is made up of a series of patterns called *rolls*. A roll is an eight-note pattern that, when combined with other rolls and some left-hand fingerings, can turn into a tune before you know it. It is vital that when you first start learning the banjo, that you learn all different variations of rolls. In this section you will learn all of the different rolls, as well as the proper fingerings for each roll.

To get a better idea of what these should sound like, each exercise and roll illustrated in this book will be demonstrated on the CD so that you can hear the sound that you are going for, and can play along with it.

A smooth, clean, and evenly played roll is the foundation of great banjo playing. I can't stress the importance of practicing the banjo roll and learning each one well before moving onto the next. When starting to learn your rolls, it is best to take the first four notes, learn them, repeat them over and over, then add the next four notes to that, and then repeat the eight-note pattern several times consecutively. It helped me when I was learning to say the number of the string I was hitting out loud as I played it. For instance, on the first roll that we are going to learn I would say "three-two-five-one-four-two-five-one" as I was hitting each string. It will take some time getting used to reading the tablature and applying it to the banjo, but take your time with each roll and make sure that you are using the correct right-hand finger on each note.

The most important thing to remember is to **take your time and go slowly**. A friend of mine shared with me a saying that his teacher told him, and that is: "If you don't know it right slow, it will be worse when it's fast." It is only natural to want to speed up when you feel yourself starting to get it, but your speed will increase naturally as you become comfortable with the rolls.

Basic Rolls

All following rolls are demonstrated on the CD at both slow (one click per eighth note) and fast tempos; they are played over an **open G chord**.

Roll 1 - Thumb In & Out Roll
"Cripple Creek" Roll (Alternating Thumb Roll)

CD Track 3

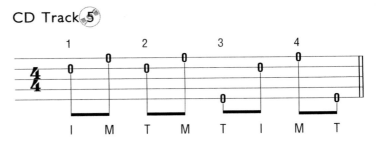

Roll 2 - Forward-Backward Roll

CD Track 4

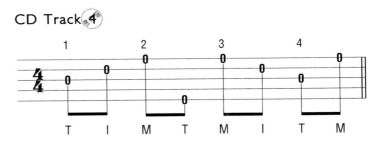

Roll 3 - Forward Roll

CD Track 5

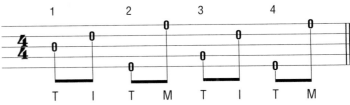

Roll 4 - Backward Roll

CD Track 6

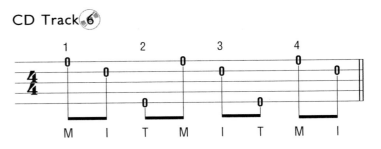

Roll 5 - Alternate Forward-Backward Roll

CD Track 7

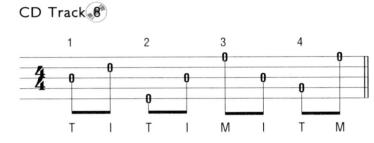

Roll 6 - Fill-In Roll

CD Track 8

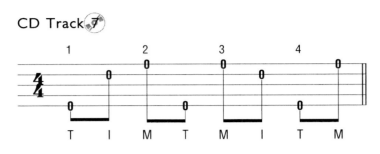

Roll 7 - Alternating Thumb Pattern

CD Track 9

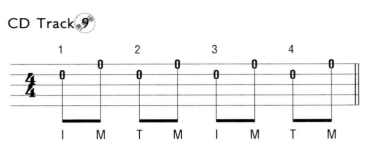

Roll 8 - Alternate Forward Roll

CD Track 10

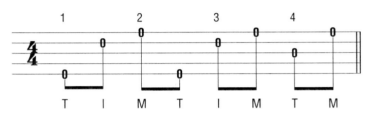

OTHER RIGHT-HAND TECHNIQUES

Pinch or Pluck

The *pinch* (or *pluck*) is played by picking two or three strings at the same time.

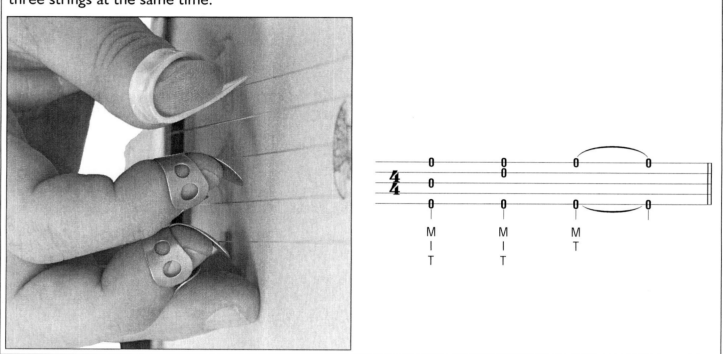

This exercise combines single notes and pinching.

CD Track H

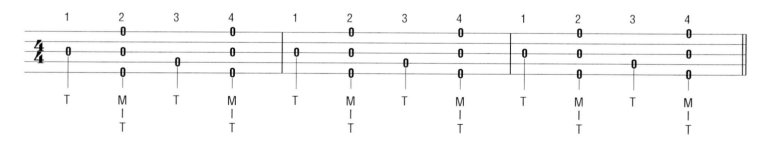

This exercise will combine the basic "thumb in and out" roll with a pinch.

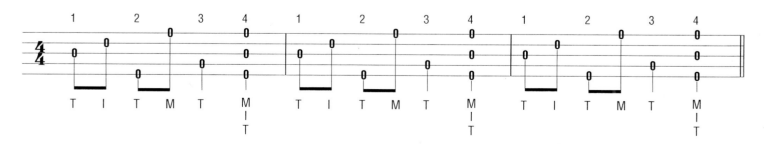

REFINING YOUR TECHNIQUE

INCORPORATING LEFT-HAND TECHNIQUES AND CHORDS

Adding Chords to the Roll

Once you have mastered the rolls and you feel that you are playing them fluently and without effort, you can start adding chords. Simply use the chords in the chord chart on page 37, and use with each roll. Make sure that when you play chords with your left hand, your fingers touch only the string indicated in the chord and you are not touching or damping other strings. This is where having your left-hand wrist in the proper position helps keep your fingers square to the fingerboard. Keep your fingers upright and perpendicular to the fingerboard and not flattened or angled. When your left hand is properly positioned, the palm part of your knuckles from your index to pinky fingers should be up against the binding of the neck.

You will see lots of people with their index palm on the neck, but at their pinky, their hand is an inch away from the neck.

It is important when doing these exercises that you change from chord to chord without hesitating or having to stop your roll to change the chord. You can take the following exercises and use them with any chord you choose. Take your time doing them slowly. As with rolls, your speed will increase naturally as you become more comfortable with changing chords.

The D7 Chord

The easiest chord to start off with will be the D7 chord. Incorporate this into your "thumb in and out" roll. Play the roll twice in open G and then play the D7 roll twice. Repeat the pattern going between open G and D7. This exercise is notated in the following tablature:

A *repeat sign* (:‖) appears at the beginning and end of a section that needs to be repeated. If the repeat sign appears only at the end of a section or song, repeat from the beginning.

CD Track 12

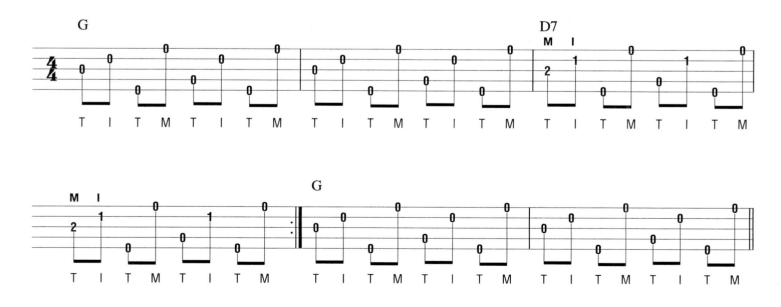

The C Chord

For this next exercise we will use a C chord and the "forward-backward" roll.

Play the roll through twice in open G and then change to your C chord, playing through the roll twice and then back to open G.

CD Track 13

23

SLIDE, HAMMER-ON, PULL-OFF, AND PUSH-OFF

Now let's move on to the more challenging left-hand techniques: the slide, the hammer-on, the pull-off, and push-off. The purpose of each of these techniques is to create the sound of two different notes when the right hand only hits the string once.

With the slide, the sound of one note moving to the other will sound just that way, like it is sliding from one to the other. The hammer-ons, pull-offs, and push-offs have distinct yet subtle differences in sound and technique.

The Slide

We will start with the *slide*. Play the third string at the second fret with the middle finger on your left hand, and pluck the string with your right. While the string is still ringing, slide your left hand up to the fourth fret. Make sure that your left hand is not grasping the neck of the banjo too tightly and that you are creating a bit of an anchor with your thumb.

Let your hand spread out a bit and move to accommodate the slide. The timing of the slide should be quick, but not so quick that you miss the sound of the string actually sliding. Hit the string on beat 1 and slide on two and repeat on beats 3 and 4:

Slide start   **Slide end**

CD Track 14

1	2	3	4	*etc.*			
M		M		M	M	M	M
2-4		2-4		2-4	2-4	2-4	2-4
T		T		T	T	T	T

Once you are comfortable with sliding your third string, let's add it into a roll. Using the "thumb in and out roll," we will do the same second-to-fourth fret slide each time we hit the third string.

It is at this point that you will really have to concentrate on the timing between your left and right hands. Your goal should be to play this sliding exercise for one or two minutes without stopping.

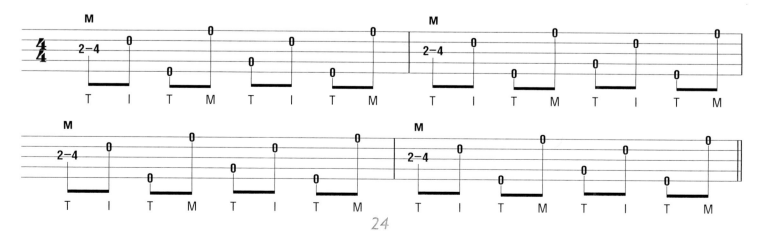

The Hammer-On

CD Track 15

Open string hammer-on

The *hammer-on* is a powerful sounding lick in banjo playing. It is important that the note rings clearly before and after it is hammered on. Your finger should act as a "hammer." When you come down on the string, be sure to hit it hard enough so that the note difference is distinct, and don't let off the string too fast. If you don't hit the string with enough force, you will deaden the sound of the note. Let's first try hammering onto the fingerboard from an open string.

Start   **End**

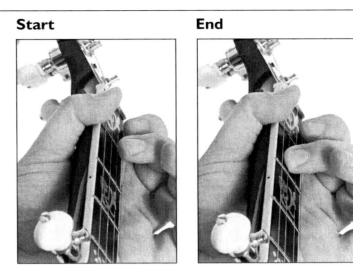

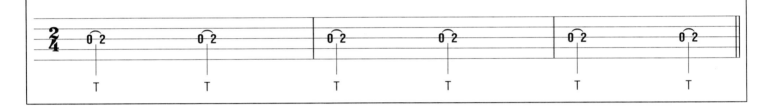

Fretted string hammer-on

Here we will hammer onto the fingerboard from a previously fretted note. Play the second string at the second fret with your first finger, and hammer onto the third fret with your middle finger.

Start   **End**

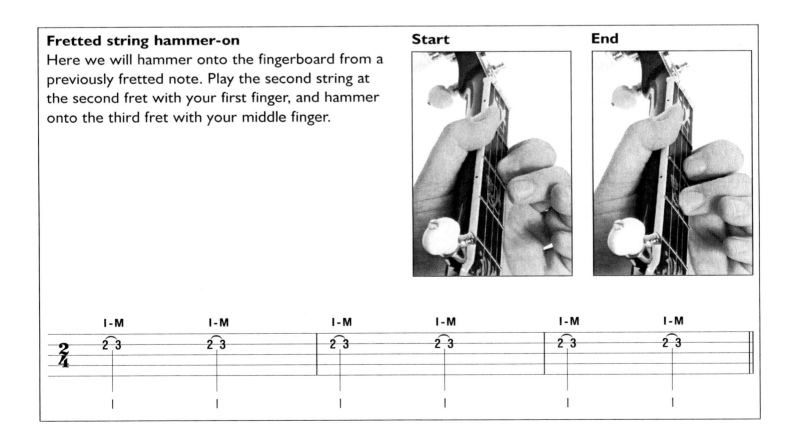

Let's do that same hammer-on in a roll. We will use a forward roll.

After you do the second hammer-on, leave your finger at the third fret until it is time to do it again.

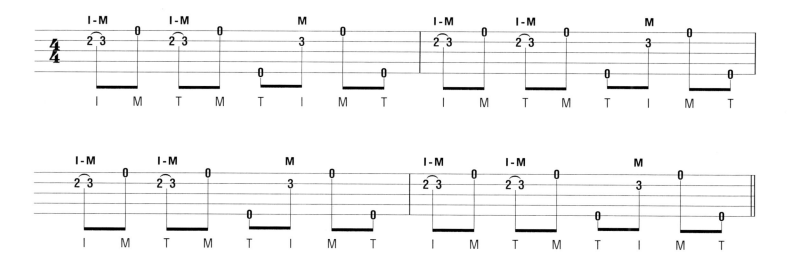

The Push-Off

The sound of a *push-off* is the opposite of a hammer-on. The note is being "pushed" and then released to a lower note. Starting with the left hand, put your index finger on the third string at the second fret and your middle finger on the same string at the third fret. Hit the string with your right hand and while the note is still ringing, push up on the string and then release it:

Push **Release**

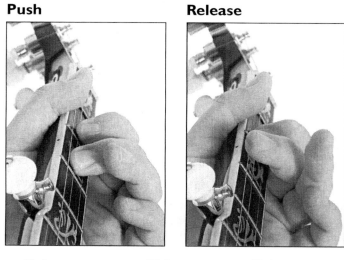

CD Track 16

Here is a simple push-off exercise doing the same push-off above on the third string:

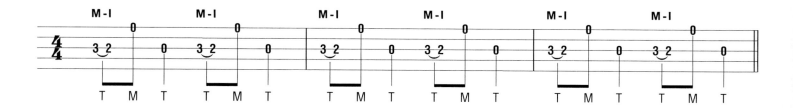

The Pull-Off

The difference between a pull-off and a push-off is that the pull-off will have a bit more of a "pop" or "snap" to the release of the string because you will use the tip of your finger and fingernail to pull the string down. Fret the notes as the push-off example on page 26, but when you release the string, pull down and release the string with a bit of a flick.

Pull   **Release**

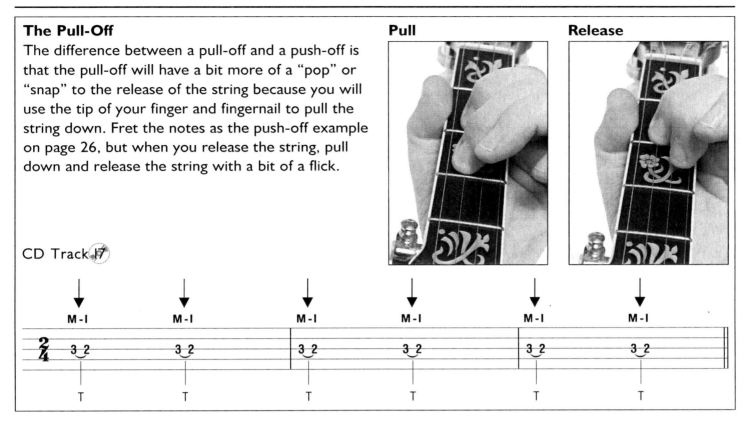

CD Track 17

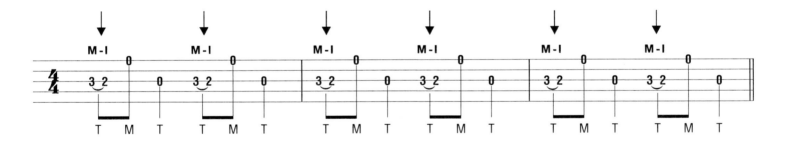

Here is a simple pull-off exercise on the third string:

PLAYING SONGS

Now for the moment that you've been waiting for! Let's get into playing some actual songs on the banjo. I have included tablature for several basic bluegrass banjo tunes using the simple right-hand patterns and left-hand techniques you have learned so far. I would advise you to listen to the songs on the CD before learning the TAB, and as you work on a song, keep referring back to the CD so that you can accustom your ear to hearing exactly what your playing should sound like.

Take each song and learn it one measure at a time, practicing that one part until you can play it smoothly, and then move onto the next measure. Rehearse that measure until you have it down and then add the two together and play them through.

Continue, one measure at a time, until you have worked your way through the entire song.

You may have the time to practice for an hour a day, every day, or you may only be able to find an hour or so a week. I've never been one to demand that a student practice for hours on end, however, I do encourage you to try to get your banjo out and play a couple of rolls or exercises for a few minutes every day, until you get the time to sit down and play for longer. A few minutes a day will keep things fresh in your mind, and in your hands as well. Do remember though, that practice makes perfect!

This arrangement is presented in the way Earl
Scruggs would play it, the [B] part as an introduction.
Enjoy!

CRIPPLE CREEK

CD Track 18

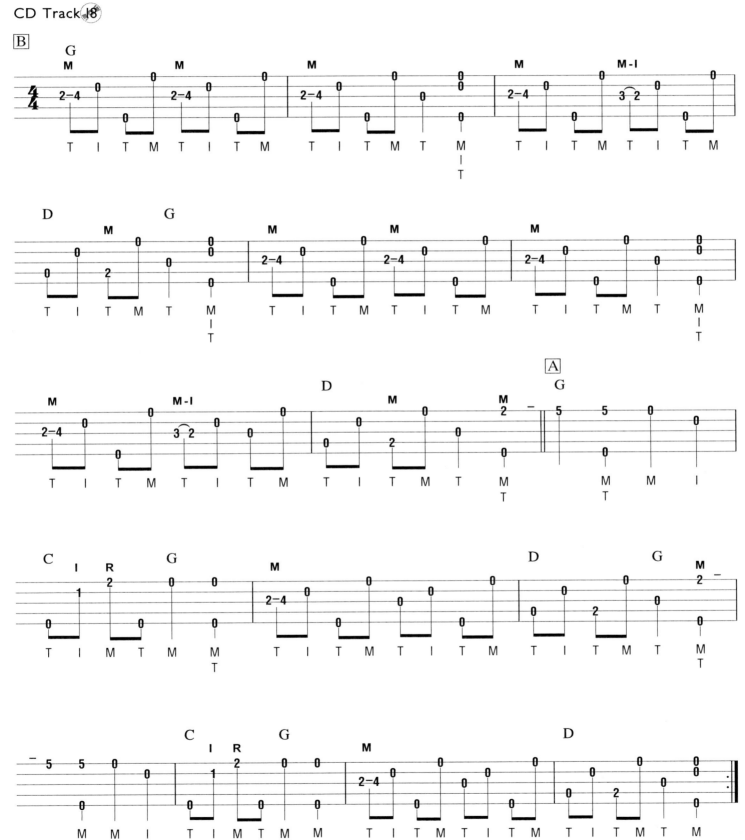

SHE'LL BE COMIN' 'ROUND THE MOUNTAIN

CD Track 19

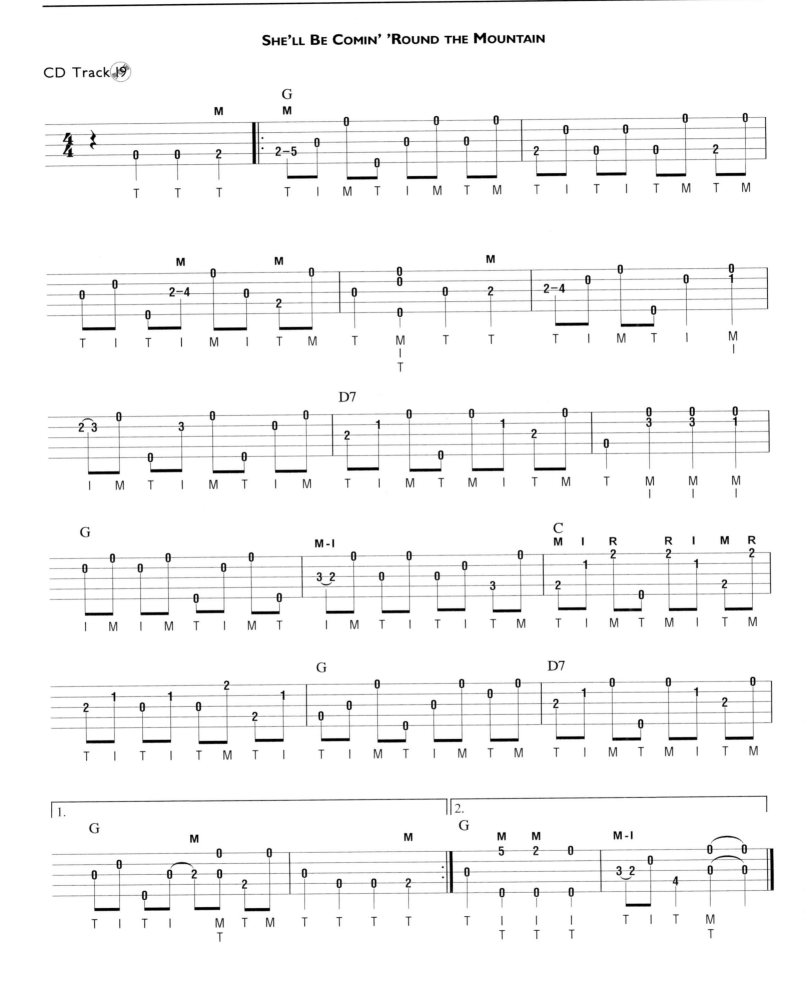

HOT CORN, COLD CORN

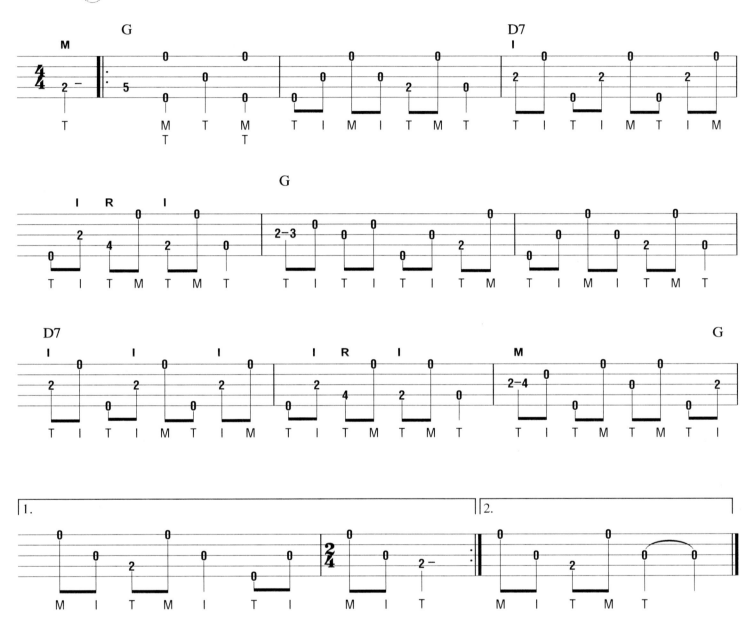

OLD JOE CLARK

CD Track 21

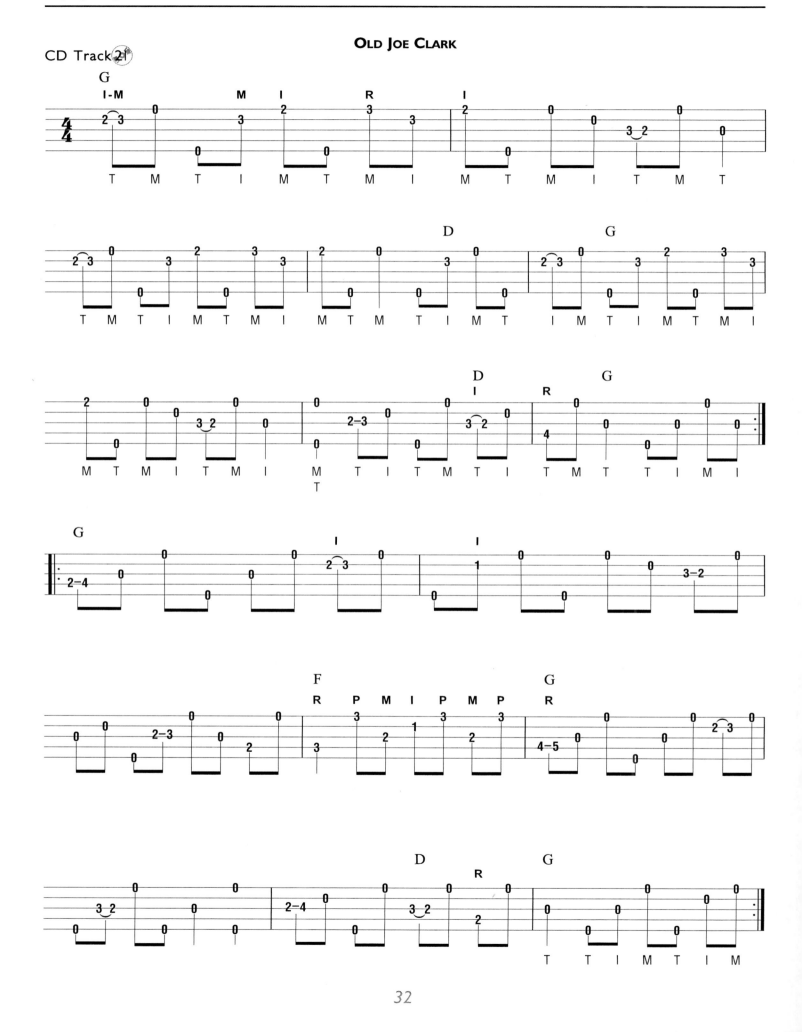

BILL CHEATHAM

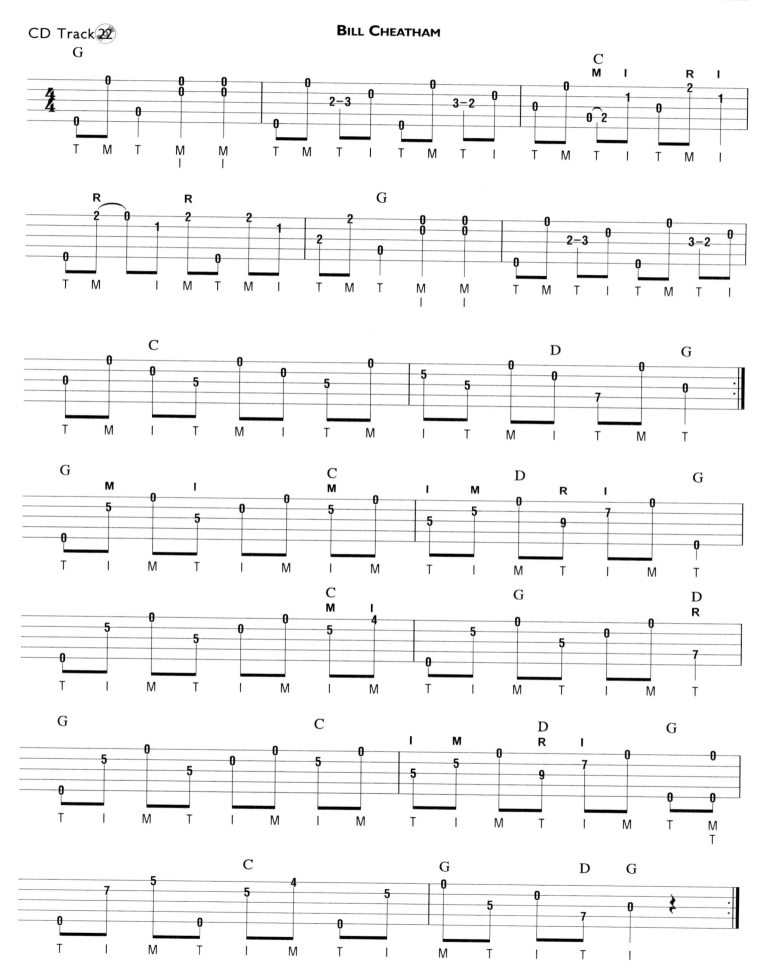

33

RED RIVER VALLEY

CD Track 23

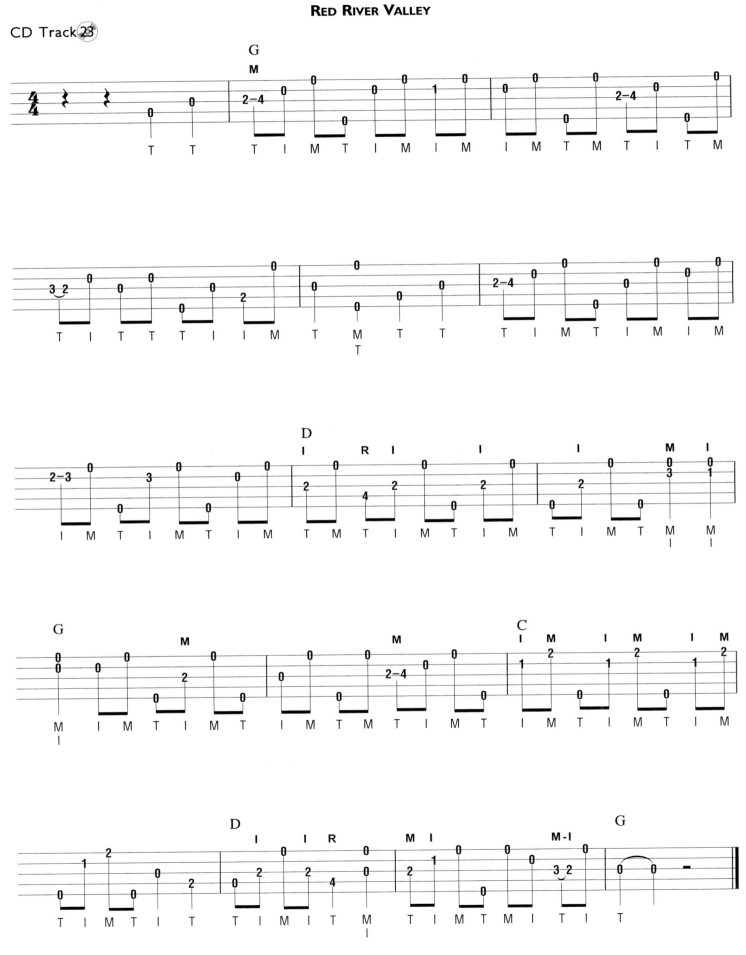

NINE POUND HAMMER

CD Track 24

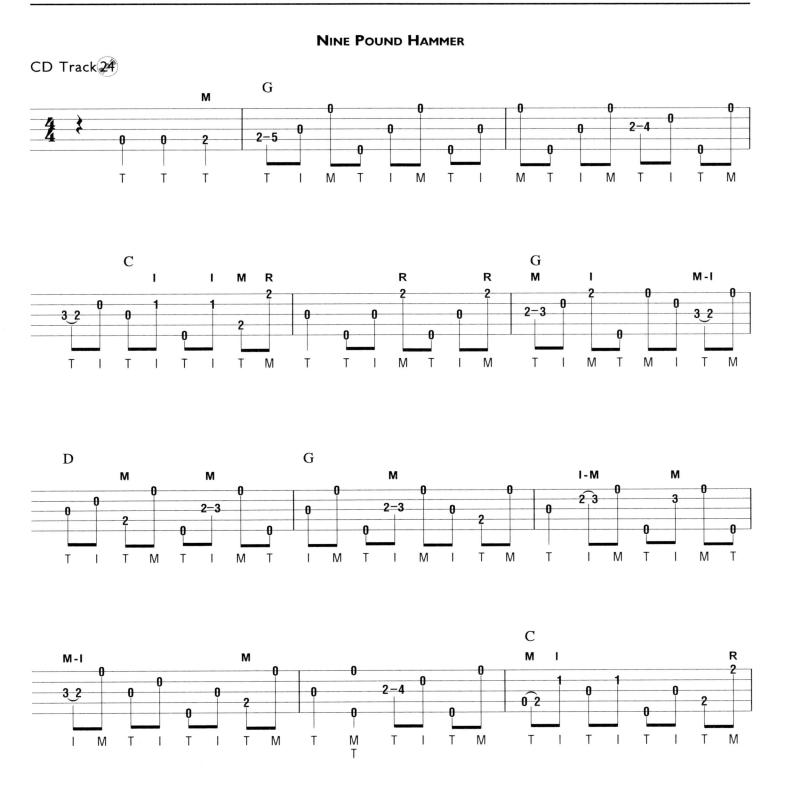

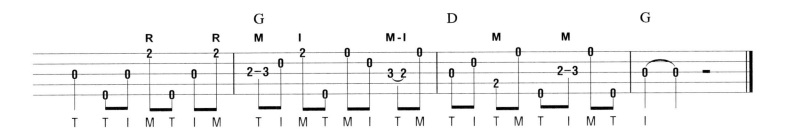

JOHN HARDY

CHORDS

Chord Diagrams

Chord diagrams are pictures of what the chords look like on the neck of the banjo. The diagrams show exactly what notes to play and what fingers to use when learning chords.

Look at the diagrams as a picture of the banjo neck facing you with the headstock pointing toward the ceiling.

The vertical lines being the strings D, G, B, and D from left to right, and the horizontal lines are the frets, with the top line as the nut unless otherwise noted. The dots are where you put your fingers, and the letter inside the dots are the fingers that you use (**I** = index, **M** = middle, **R** = ring and **P** = pinky). An "O" above the string indicates that the string is open.

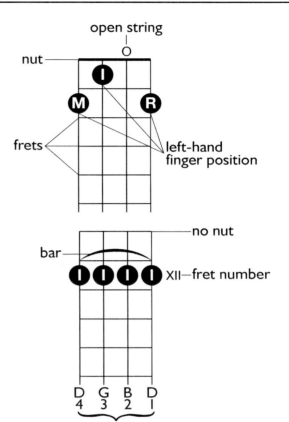

G
Open

G

G

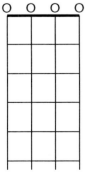

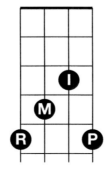

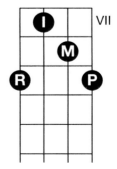

G	G	C

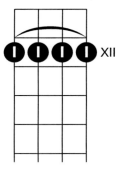

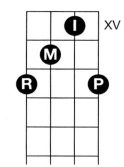

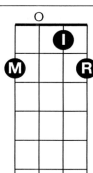

C	C	C
Position 2	Position 3	Position 4

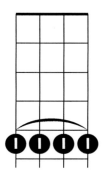

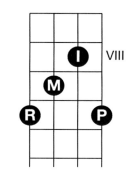

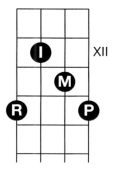

D7

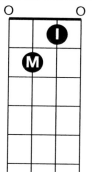

D

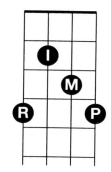

D
Position 2

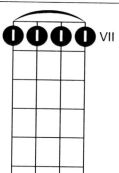

D
Position 3

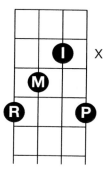

D
Position 4

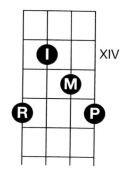

E

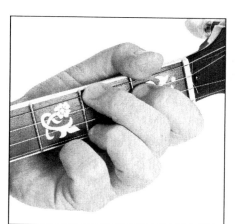

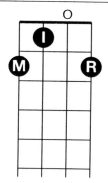

E
Position 2

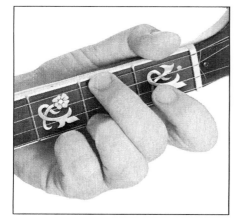

E
Position 3

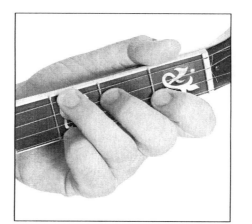

E
Position 4

Em

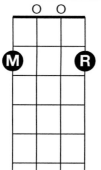

F

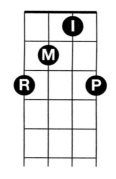

F
Position 2

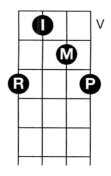

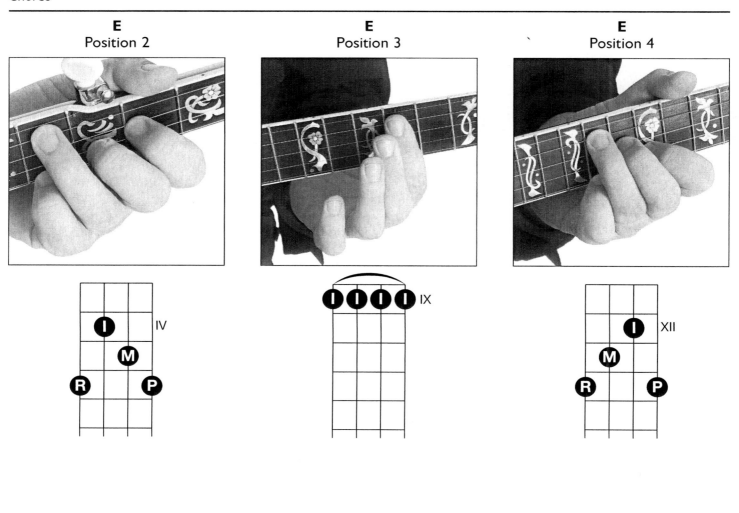

F
Position 3

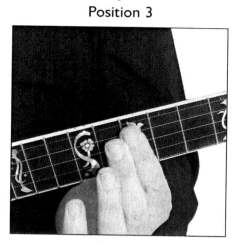

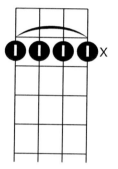

A

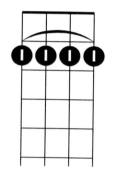

A
Position 2

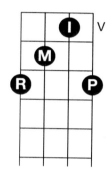

B

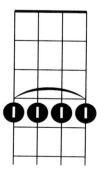

B
Position 2

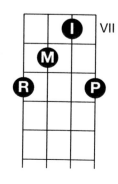

B7

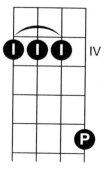

BANJO MAINTENANCE

If you have recently purchased your banjo from a music store, ask them if they could recommend someone who could help you with setting up your instrument and show you how to do it yourself. Once a banjo has been set up properly, there is rarely any maintenance that you will need to do aside from changing the strings.

Here are a few tips on setting up your banjo that will help with the tuning and tone of your instrument.

The Head

A brand new banjo straight from the factory may not have a very tight head. The tightness of the head affects the tone of the banjo. If it is too loose, the banjo will sound dull and soft. If it is too tight, the banjo will be too bright and not have an even tone. Push down on the head with your thumb gently but firmly. You want a little bit of resistance, but your thumb should not sink into the head very much. I tune my banjo head according to the sound that I hear and like to come from my banjo. Some tune the head to a G or an A by listening to the tone of the head. Tap the head softly and listen for the tones that will ring naturally. If you don't have much of a ring, you may want to tighten the head.

To tune the head, use the metal key that comes with your banjo Depending on the type of banjo, take the back off and, using the key, start at 1 o'clock and then 7 o'clock, 2 o'clock and then 8 o'clock, and so on, and go around the banjo, tightening the keys no more than $\frac{1}{8}$ of a turn. Go completely around the head once, put the back on, tap for tone, and play it a bit. Repeat if you feel it is necessary.

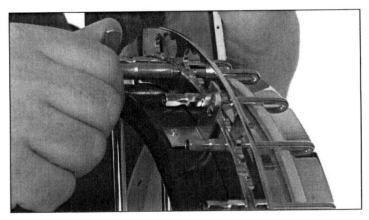

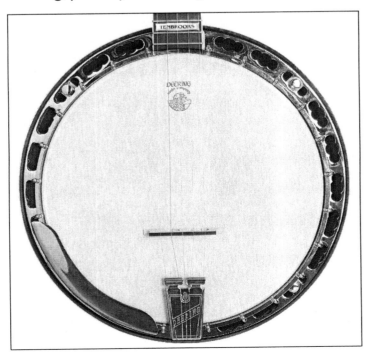

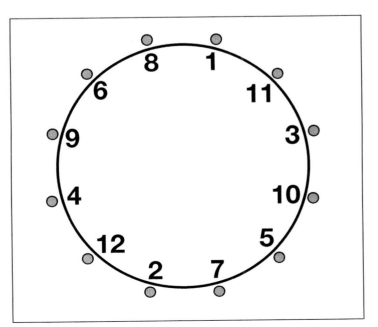

The Bridge

The bridge holds the strings up from the head of the banjo. Your banjo will come with one, but in the rare case that it should break or crack, you can purchase a new one from any music store. The taller the bridge, the further the strings are from the neck and the louder your banjo will be. A standard ⅝" height bridge will do fine. The bridge should be placed directly in the center of the head so that the third string, coming out of the tailpiece, goes straight up the neck to the nut.

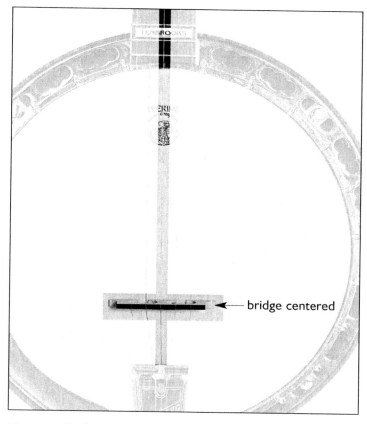

bridge centered

You can find the correct placement for the bridge by measuring between the nut and the bridge. The twelfth fret is technically the halfway point between the bridge and nut. Measure accordingly for both sides of the bridge.

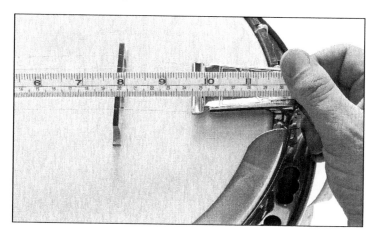

Mark the head around the feet of the bridge with a pencil after you have found the correct placement so that if the bridge ever moves, you won't have to measure again to find the right spot.

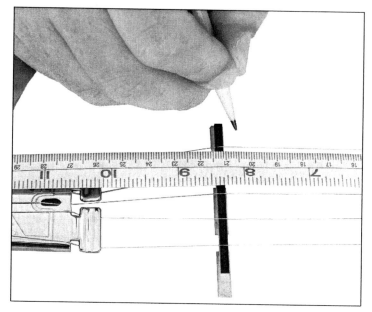

After placing the bridge, tune your banjo to the tuner and check the *harmonic* of each string at the twelfth fret. Harmonics are easy to produce: touch a string with your middle finger very lightly at the twelfth fret, then strum the string with your right hand.

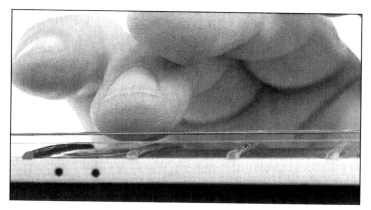

If you are touching the string the right way, it will make a "chime." Chime the string at the twelfth fret and then play it the regular way at the twelfth fret. If the fretted note is lower than the chime, slightly move the bridge up, or toward the neck. If the fretted note is higher, move the bridge back towards the tailpiece. Keep repeating this until the chime and the fretted note match. You will find that the first, second, and fourth strings will get in tune, but the third may be just a tiny bit out. Some prefer to use a bridge with a cut-out for the third string to compensate for this intonation.

Strings

How often you should change strings is up to you. If you are someone who has clammy or sweaty palms, you may very well deaden a set of strings within a few days of playing. Some people can go for a month or more until the string dies naturally. On average, you may want to change strings once or twice a month if you are playing on a daily basis.

Depending on your local music store, you may have little choice in string brands. I prefer GHS "Almost Medium" strings. The gauges are .10, .11, .13, .20, and .10 (first string to fifth string). However, I think you will find any pack of strings around this gauge very comfortable.

It doesn't matter which string you start with, but don't ever remove them all at once because you want the tension of the strings to keep the bridge securely in place.

How to Change Your Strings

1. Lift the tailpiece cover and remove the old string. Start by loosening it by detuning it and then just unwrap the string with your hand.

2. Take the new string and hook the loop end in the appropriate place in the tailpiece.

3. Thread the other end of the string into the post. There will be more string than you actually need.

4. Pull the string through and give yourself about an inch or more of slack in the string.

5. Using your right hand to hold the string in place tightly at the post, use your left hand to turn the peg.

Remember that the fourth and third strings will turn upwards, and the first and second strings will turn downwards. You want the string to wrap around the peg about four times so that it won't slip. Use your tuner and tune this string accordingly. Using wire cutters, snip off any extra. It will take time to perfect changing the strings, but you'll get it.

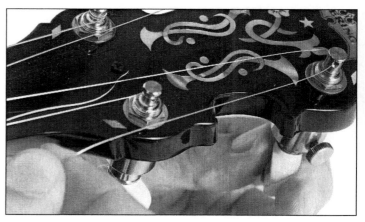

I try not to be a banjo guru when it comes to my instrument. When I experience any problem with it, I take it to someone who is learned in instrument repair and setup. I liken it to going to the doctor, or taking your car to a mechanic.

APPENDIX I: BLUEGRASS RESOURCES

Listening Suggestions

I can't stress enough the importance of listening to different banjo players as well as bluegrass music in general. Unless you already have a favorite banjo player whose style appeals to you, get out there and hear and see as many players as you can. There are so many different styles of banjo playing and it's important to hear each one and draw from them—not only for the style, but the difference in tone and technique that is unique to each player and their instrument.

I was schooled in the "Scruggs" style of playing and to this day Earl Scruggs remains my favorite player and main influence.

However, I remember hearing Sonny Osborne for the first time and recognizing the difference in his "sound" compared to what I had been used to listening to. The same goes for J.D. Crowe, Ralph Stanley, and Allen Shelton, to name a few.

There are so many tools available in this day and age for learning and listening, that they are almost too numerous to mention. The Internet has opened up a whole new world of resources for the banjo—from banjo chat rooms, to video lessons, not to mention an extensive library of songs to download. Here are a few recordings, old and new, that I think will give you a good variety of styles and banjo "sounds."

Recordings

Flatt, Lester and Scruggs, Earl. *Foggy Mountain Banjo* (County 100)

Bluegrass Album Band. *The Bluegrass Album,* Volumes 1–4 (Rounder 140, 164, 180, and 210)

Osborne Brothers. *Once More,* Volumes 1 & 2 (Sugar Hill 2203)

Reno, Don. *Fastest Five Strings Alive* (Hollywood 227)

Fleck, Bela. *Drive* (Rounder 225)

Mills, Jim. *My Dixie Home* (Sugar Hill 3951)

For those of you who are good at finding your way around on a computer, try checking out these sites:

www.banjohangout.org

www.banjonews.com

Check out your local newspapers and see if there are any local bluegrass venues where you can go and see someone perform. You might even find that they have a jam session a night or two a month. It only helps to further your playing to be around other players, have them show you things, or to just talk banjo!

APPENDIX II: BANJO HUMOR

Your only defense as a banjo player is to know every banjo joke out there and react with little or no emotion when you hear one.

Why banjo players have become the brunt of such distasteful humor is hard to say, because we ALL know that if it wasn't for the banjo, it wouldn't be bluegrass!

What's the difference between a banjo... and a chainsaw?

> *answer:*   The chainsaw has dynamic range.

the South-American Macaw?

> *answer:*   One is loud, obnoxious and noisy; the other is a bird.

an onion?

> *answer:*   Nobody cries when you cut up a banjo.

How many banjo players does it take to screw in a lightbulb?

> *answer:*   Five! One to screw it in and four to:
> complain that it's electric.
> lament about how much they miss the old one.
> argue about how Earl would have done it.
> argue about what year it was made.
> argue about how much it cost.

How can you tell if the stage is level?

> *answer:*   Drool will run out of both sides of the banjo player's mouth.

Why do some people take an instant aversion to banjo players?

> *answer:*   It saves time in the long run.

What do you call a good musician at a banjo contest?

> *answer:*   A visitor.

What is the one thing that you'll never hear anybody ever say?

> *answer:*   That's the banjo player's Porsche.

How can you make a thousand dollars playing the banjo?

> *answer:*   Start out with two thousand.

How many banjo jokes are there?

> *answer:*   Only three, the rest are true stories!

ABOUT THE AUTHOR

Robin has been a professional banjo player and teacher for over twenty years. Robin has been part of many recognized bluegrass and country bands, including: Petticoat Junction, Wild & Blue, Blue & Lonesome, Twisted Lester, Bull Harman & Bull's Eye, and Mixt Company. Robin has also played with Bill Monroe, Jim and Jesse McReynolds, Charlie Louvin, and Jimmy Martin. Robin lives in Nashville, Tennessee.

Also from the Oak
BANJO COLLECTION

The Banjo Picker's Fakebook
By David Brody
The ultimate sourcebook for banjo players! Contains over 230 jigs, reels, rags, hornpipes, and breakdowns from all major traditional instrumental styles. Includes discography and special introductory materials on regional styles, interpretation and bluegrass techniques.

ISBN 0.8256.0271.8
UPC 7.52187.64261.9
OK64261

The Banjo Player's Songbook
By Tim Jumper
Arranged for the five-string banjo in easy-to-play tablature, every style of music is represented in this giant volume of over 200 songs. Includes lyrics to folk songs, sentimental favorites, holiday songs, sing-alongs, and more!

ISBN 0.8256.0297.1
UPC 7.52187.64709.6
OK64709

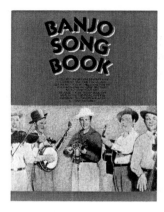

Banjo Song Book
By Tony Trischka
A thorough survey of the three-finger picking classics of the early 1900s, transitional styles of the 1930s, the Scruggs style of the 1940s, and beyond! There are instructional sections on Scruggs, Reno, and melodic picking, plus more than 75 tunes in tablature.

ISBN 0.8256.0197.5
UPC 7.52187.63438.6
OK63438

Bluegrass Banjo
By Peter Wernick
Thirty-five songs offering a complete exploration of bluegrass music. Includes music theory, tips on performance, bluegrass ensemble playing, back-up playing, and a wealth of banjo lore. Features "Oh Susannah," "Skip To My Lou," and more! For beginners and advanced players.

Book and CD
ISBN 0.8256.0148.7
UPC 7.52187.62778.4
OK62778

Melodic Banjo
By Tony Trischka
A complete instruction guide to "Keith style" banjo technique. Over 30 tunes and songs by Bill Keith, Eric Weissberg, Alan Munde, Bobby Thompson, Vic Jordan, and others. Contains descriptions of their personal playing styles as well as interviews.

Book and CD
ISBN 0.8256.0171.1
UPC 7.52187.63149.1
OK63149

Banjo Case Chord Book
By Larry Sandberg
Find the banjo chords you need instantly! This handy manual is conveniently sized at 4.5 by 12 inches, allowing you to take it everywhere. The book includes many fingerings for each chord, charts for using chords in any key, a complete tuning chart, and more!

ISBN 0.8256.2377.4
UPC 7.52187.34885.6
AM34885

Oak Publications
A part of *The* **Music Sales** *Group*